MATT'S MYSTIC MANDALAS

The Last Oneironaut

ISBN: 978-0-692-99467-2

ISBN-10:069299467x

I would like to thank my parents for always having my back
I would also like to thank my friends for
being with me on this journey.

This book is dedicated to Ed and Helen for taking me to all of those museums
In the city as a kid, and showing me that pursuing art is a lifelong endeavor.

For thousands of years, mandalas have been used as a tool to achieve enlightenment by tapping into a higher consciousness within. Crafting and coloring mandalas allows one to become completely absorbed by the intrinsic beauty of these creations; all thoughts and worries subside as the peace and tranquility of the present moment expands. Through repetition and focus, their healing and transformative nature can begin to affect the very essence of your being. By tuning into the divine presence that lies dormant within all of us we can reach a state of bliss, despite daily troubles.

In 2013 at the age of 20, I began researching mandalas and learned about their transformative powers. Soon after, I made the decision to begin creating them as an extension of my meditation. Freeing myself from the stream of thoughts constantly running through my head seemed nearly impossible, but I had nothing to lose so I started from the center, and began my journey. As I practiced, I grew confident that the mandala was indeed having a positive effect on my state of mind, and soon realized using them could be the greatest asset on my path to inner peace. If I could calm the daily bombardment of information that threatens to unbalance my mind, body, and soul, then I could take that same practice with me everywhere I go and improve my overall well being while helping others along the way.

As you begin to color…notice that no mandala is perfectly geometric. I used no rulers, protractors, or compasses when creating this book: in fact, I've never used a measuring device to make any mandala. I made this decision upon beginning my journey to acknowledge my humanity and express "perfect imperfection." My mandalas are an honest expression of my own accomplishments and mistakes, both of which are equally important. By sharing them with you, we can move together toward the realization that each mistake brings us closer to the blessing of true peace found within.

Do not dwell in the past; do not dream of the future,
concentrate the mind on the present moment

Buddhist proverb

PROTECTION WISD

DISCIPLINE

"May all beings have happy minds"
The Buddha